Collectors'

Antics

Published by Owl Press, P.O. Box 315 Downton, Salisbury, Wilts. SP5 3YE 1994
Printed in the UK by BPC Wheatons Ltd, Exeter.

British Library Cataloguing - in - Publication data. A catalogue record for this book
is available from the British Library.

Publisher's ISBN: 1 898052 25 5

Collectors'
Antics

Les Lilley & David Downe

About the Authors

LES LILLEY is the writer and deviser of many cartoon strips including most of those from the Disney stable and, currently, *Tom and Jerry* for worldwide syndication, the librettos for two 'musicals', both produced but both flops, and hundreds of shows for both TV and radio - *Vision On, The Golden Shot* and *Beyond Belief* being those that spring most readily to mind. He has also written gags and texts for an endless stream of cartoon books produced in collaboration with various cartoonists of note.

This is the first time he has worked with David Downe and he is hoping to recoup a little of the money he has frittered away at Boot Fairs and Antique Markets over his many years as a collector of totally worthless bric-a-brac.

DAVID DOWNE was born, chuckling, during the depression of 1931 and is still smiling. He was educated at St Edwards, Oxford and the Royal Military Academy, Sandhurst. He was commissioned in 1951, 'retired' in 1968 and became variously thereafter, unemployed for one blissful year, a freelance cartoonist in Fleet Street and ultimately Director of the West Midlands Area Museum Service.

During his career as a cartoonist he has contributed to the cartoon columns of most of the popular and less popular press as well as to specialist collections. Now retired from the museum service, he has returned to drawing cartoons. In 1993 he wrote and illustrated *A Regimental Mess*, a collection which explores the prospects for redundancy and resettlement in the Services. He has recently published *Diary of a Dogsbody* which examines the pleasures and pitfalls of owning a dog.

He first met Les Lilley during the late '60s at the King Leo Agency. They immediately established a genial air of amiable compatibility and rapport which lasted down the years to the production of *Collectors' Antics*.

Foreword

In my opinion there is no better way of spending a spare Sunday than trolling slowly round an Antiques Fair, finding something you are able to convince yourself you need and fooling yourself into believing you can afford it. This is the modus operandi of the true collector.

Some may classify the true collector as the knowledgable pedant whose sole purpose in visiting an Antiques Fair must be to recognise quality, know its price, and to haggle with tressle-tabled traders 'til he or she gains a palpable victory and leaves the hall having paid a mere fifty pounds for something that is obviously worth fifty-one pounds. But this is not the way in which I would define my compulsion. Such cheeseparing exactitude would, in my opinion, take the fun out of taking a chance.

The true collector, rather like a compulsive gambler, spends his life poking around stalls, shops, boot fairs, antique fairs and street markets in the hope that he will one day achieve 'The Big Bargain'. That he will pick up for fifty pence something that will one day be featured on the *Antiques Road Show* and later be knocked down in auction for hundreds of thousands of pounds at Sotheby's.

Let's face it, looking for antiques, or collectables, or even bits and pieces of last year's rubbish is more an entertainment than a commercial venture for the likes of most of us.

Well, if it's not, it jolly well should be!

Les Hilley

Antique Hunters & Punters

The dear litle old lady

Dealers should beware of these. Some are as harmless as they look, while others have minds like steel traps, the persistence of a hungry alligator, possibly a better idea of the value of your stock than you and a thriving business exporting quality antiques to the Middle East.

The fraught mother

A fully agitated one of these has the destructive capabilities of a nuclear strike. Its umbrella and packages have a devastating effect on glass and china while childlike appendages have been known to dent armour and knock fifty per cent off the value of cast iron door-stops merely by touching them. There is only one defence against such a threat - early closing!

The know-it-all

This character will inspect your stock and inform you that he has more and better in his attic. His 'expert' knowledge is based on the fact that he once attended an auction, has read a book on old furniture and regularly watches the *Antiques Road Show*. Suitably flattered, he can usually be persuaded to pay high prices for anything that remotely resembles his own possessions, this being his expensive method of establishing quotable prices for rubbish when boasting about it to his friends and neighbours.

The nouveau stall holder

He has been edged into a new line of salesmanship by economic recession. He previously spent thirty years extolling the virtues of, and selling, used cars. He therefore has vast experience as a salesman and is convinced he can sell anything. In reality his sheer aggressiveness so frightens potential customers that fall-out from his patter has been known even to force owners of stalls adjacent to his into bankruptcy!

The over-enthusiastic customer

This is an extremely agitated customer, usually very attractive in a sexy way. She gets so interested in almost unreachable items of your stock that she completely distracts your attention from her confederate (plain and unsexy) who will plunder the best pieces at the other end of your counter, table or car blanket. Items lost to such a predatory client should be written off against education, though not necessarily education pertaining to any form of antiquity.

The diffident dealer

He seems not to care whether or not he sells. It is difficult to attract his attention as he is seemingly engrossed in much more pressing business than ever could be offered by you, a mere customer. In reality he has a mind like a gimlet and will empty your wallet should you show the slightest interest in purchasing his wares. He usually drives a twelve year old Ford Estate but takes his holidays (twice yearly) on the Island of Mustique.

Collecting Glass

The collection of glass is a fascinating pastime. No collectable is more broadly based. Glass ranges from ancient ginger beer bottles rescued from rubbish tips, runs the gamut of Nailsea walking sticks, bad-taste Friggers, and American pressings eventually to arrive at the top end of the market among the wonders and splendours of Lalique, Waterford and Baccarat.

Glass is possibly the most seductive of all collectables, but the golden rule of this particular discipline should always be observed: ANTIQUE GLASS AND CHILDREN DO NOT CO-EXIST! Small children are possibly responsible for the very high price of fine glass. There would be more of it about were it not for the elbows of infants. Its price would consequently be reduced in accordance with its lack of rarity. This fact is recognised as being the first dynamic of the law of breakages.

Given a relatively decorous household, a collector manqué may gain much delight from his or her glass. It is easy to display in the context of even a home furnished in the most modern manner. Good glass is useful as tableware, it is useful as a receptacle, and a floral display can only enhance the most esoteric acquisition.

It should be noted, however, that certain items have limited use. It would be silly to assume that flowers would look good in a ginger beer bottle, and even the most elegant piece of crystal will go for nothing if used as a bowl for the dog's drinking water.

Discretion and a sense of style coupled with careful family planning should be your watchwords.

"These Nailsea walking sticks are very collectable, but if you want a real rarity we have a Nailsea glass zimmer frame."

"This is a thistle glass with a domed foot and two shoulder knops and I'd say, - not only is it twentieth century but you should return it to the saloon bar before it closes."

"When the dealer told me it was a specimen bottle, I thought it was designed to take a single rose!"

"The chandelier cost so much at auction we couldn't afford to move it to the larger house we originally bought it for."

"If he asks the price of that pair of crystal candlesticks say, 'Eighty pounds' - if he doesn't flinch say, 'Each' - and if he still doesn't flinch say, 'Plus VAT'."

"Of course you can't see anything through it. I told you it belonged to Admiral Lord Nelson!"

"A few spots on a mirror are a bit of a plus factor especially if they draw attention away from the spots on a punter's face."

"Trade is so bad he's accumulated a wonderful collection of Guiness bottles while trying to drown his sorrows."

"Of course her diamonds aren't real - the last time she dropped one she had seven years bad luck!"

"I warned him that adding the price tag to the chandelier would be the last straw!"

Furniture

It is an oft stated fact that it is, in the long term, cheaper to buy an antique than new furniture. Theory has it that new furniture loses half its value once taken from the showroom, whereas the antique will increase in value with every passing day of being sat upon or otherwise used.

I emphasise that this is only theory, because old furniture can be a bad bargain if it falls to pieces the first time it is sat upon. It can be an even worse bargain if riddled with woodworm and results in your home falling apart. 'Caveat emptor', is the legal phrase that covers these contingencies. Let the buyer beware.

So make sure your newly acquired mid-Victorian Davenport with rococo scroll supports is strong enough to support its own rococos. Check that your ten foot long late seventeenth century solid oak dresser isn't too heavy for your early twentieth century floorboards with their added dry rot. And make sure also that your bargain walnut veneered two-part bureau isn't about to fall into seven or eight parts.

Having found yourself a reputable dealer, made all the necessary checks, and bought your piece at a fair price, it is now reasonably certain that you will be able to spend many years sitting in a vastly uncomfortable chair, easing your agony with the certain knowledge that you are at least keeping pace with the inflationary spiral.

"All roll-tops have secret drawers - but they wouldn't be secret if we knew where they were, would they?"

"If this is really a commode, can you demonstrate where and how one sits?"

"Do you think perhaps it's a soupçon over-restored for a Queen Anne Swan Back, Albert?"

31

"It comes with a certificate of authenticity signed by the Managing Director of Plantaganet Antiques guaranteeing that this is the *very* bed in which Henry the Eighth discovered the Divine Right of Kings!"

"Oh, I wasn't bidding - just letting the owner of the chair know that I had finished pushing her price up!"

"Here we are, Ma'am. - a six foot long Victorian brass bedstead - only partly used by a four foot six Victorian jockey."

"All genuine antique chairs have uneven legs, Madam. They were made that way to compensate for uneven floors."

"Of course it isn't a genuine Jacobean TV cabinet - it's a reproduction of a genuine Jacobean TV cabinet!"

"This is a late Georgian chest, 'improved' by the Victorians and therefore considerably less valuable than it would have been had the whiskery idiots left it alone!"

"Now that's what I call an Archbishop of Canterbury's Canterbury!"

"This Louis XV sideboard is a trifle too large. Do you have a Louis XIV?"

Boot Fairs

If fifteen years ago the man in the street had been asked to define a 'Boot Fair' he would probably thought it to be a gathering of cobblers, rather than the load of cobblers and unwanted household dross that is sold on such occasions.

From a standing start such events have proliferated like fungus and are in the process of covering every sports field throughout the length and breadth of the land - mostly on Sunday mornings.

A visit to a Boot Fair on a Sunday morning has now become a social occasion that has outstripped the traditional visit to church in popularity. In fact, some churches actually organise Boot Fairs to find the money to maintain and repair their fabric, so ensuring a place of worship should its parishioners one day tire of Sunday markets and return to the fold.

Boot Fairs have been found to be particularly addictive. It is not unknown for the customers of Boot Fairs to acquire so many 'bargains' that their own attics start to fill to the point of overflowing. At this point they sometimes themselves become 'dealers'. In other words, 'What goes around, comes around'. The Boot Fair being the most positive form of recycling yet known to man.

"How much for the table?"

"There's no point in looking for anything specific. It's best to rely on impulse buying and the ability to match our needs to our purchases."

"Don't ask me what it is. I wouldn't be selling the thing if I knew that!"

"How can I be prosecuted under the Trade Descriptions Act when the damm' thing is indescribable anyway?"

"I was always told, 'One person's rubbish is another person's collectable'. You seemed to have proved that old saying wrong."

"That is a genuine Georgian Quizzing Glass, madam. Known in the trade as a sneer on a stick."

"Delia, you didn't, by any chance, sell a car wheel and a jack?!"

"It's a complete white elephant, luv, but I know you'll just love it when you see it."

"You won't find no date mark on the bottom of they gnomes, Missus - you 'as to calculate their ages by the length of their beards."

"Would you believe it? - some stupid punter has managed to break my sign!"

Antique Markets

Antique Markets differ from Boot Fairs in a number of ways. Firstly, the Boot Fair features 'old stuff', whereas the Antique Fair pupports to feature 'quality' old stuff. Though it is sometimes hard to understand the aesthetic difference between a second hand lawn mower and a Victorian pickle jar when the intrinsic value of a hunk of old iron is often four times that of a chunk of glass.

Antique Markets are usually held indoors and this comfort factor is all important, especially on a cold day. The warmth of a school hall tends to enhance the desirability of the goods on display, while chill winds whistling around a Boot Sale in a school playground can often lead to impulse buying on a scale that is later regretted. Antique Markets can therefore be seen to be the stamping ground of the more fastidious, the more genteel and the less hardy of collectors.

They are the happy-hunting-grounds of 'specialists'. People who collect specific items like Clarice Cliff tea services, glass marbles, cigarette cards or wartime identity cards. It is almost impossible to attend an Antiques Market without something catching a collector's eye'.

Moorcroft pottery and Wedgewood ashtrays abound. Service medals from World War I proliferate alongside enough strings of Whitby jet to reach from here to the moon. There are also enough chipped and battered Dinky toys to cause gridlock on the M25.

It is as if manufacturers from past generations deliberately produced an excess of bits and pieces that was intended to provide stock for the bric-a-brac dealers of today. This has led to a sameness in Antiques Markets that is only offset and made tolerable by slight regional fluctuations in price.

It used to be that bargain hunters at Antiques Markets in the North of England got slightly better bargains than their fellow hunters in the South. But once the secret was out, news of bargain antiques that could be picked up for a "snip" spread like wildfire. The consequent rush of shoppers from the South heading north of the Wash resulted in a steep rise in prices to counter the unexpected demand. My advice is simple, if you happen upon a source of underpriced antiques, keep it strictly to yourself. For once the word gets out you will find yourself joining the queue behind a stream of dealers' vans.

"*There is a great demand for teapots that don't look like teapots. I spent most of yesterday evening trying to get a mouthful of Earl Grey out of my wife's sewing machine!*"

"I've seen a great many artificially distressed sideboards but this is going to ridiculous extremes!"

"I'm getting much too old for this business."

"The machine isn't for sale, Sir. What I do sell is old pennies that fit it - at a quid each!"

"I don't know what came over me. I only went into the place to shelter from the rain!"

"Would you mind accompanying me to the Manager's office, Madam?"

"- Lot 55...18th century Sedan Chair, low mileage, original leather seats fitted with chastity belts."

"She is extremely déclassé, my dear. Rumour has it that her tiara came from an Oxfam shop!"

"I believe such beads were called mourning jewellery because Victorian wives were seldom allowed to buy such trinkets when their husbands were alive!"

"I want to make a really good investment. Do you have anything on offer for which you don't know the true value?"

Art Galleries & Art

When I was very, very young I was intimidated by art galleries. I used to peer through their plate glass windows trying to see the pictures on exhibition within, put off from closer inspection by the rarified ambience of the places and the incredible aloofness of the well-groomed, skinny men and women who presided over these small temples given over to the worship of artistic talent.

Then a close relative became the manager of such a gallery and I learned that the buying and selling of art in such a way is only a few steps removed from the buying and selling of used cars and probably as risky if you are looking for 'The Big Bargain'.

It isn't really necessary to have a vast knowledge of art and artists in order to buy well. If you look at a painting and like it so much that you feel you could live with it hanging over your chimney breast for the rest of your life, then go for it. Even if you later discover it to be worthless, you will still have something hanging on your wall that you can enjoy.

Whatever else you do, it is bad thinking to buy something you dislike merely because you think it to be underpriced and a bargain. If it turns out to be not worth much at all, then your bargain immediately becomes rubbish!

"Have you noticed how they seem to point at you no matter where you stand in the gallery?"

"- and a ransom note for £50,000 in used furniture and unmarked silver or they will never see their Madonna again without a moustache."

"If you will just saw the painting across the middle for me I can sell it as a pair."

"I'm sorry Mr Hals, there's no call for Laughing Cavaliers nowadays. Do a couple of dozen miserable ones and we could do business."

"Must they use the Van Dyke, Officer?"

"More limited edition Art Nouveau than Collectable Erotica - I would say."

" - under the Trades Descriptions Act, did you offer Van Gogh's ear for sale at the reduced price of £2,000 for half a dozen?"

"What exactly are they pre-raffling?"

"This Constable is so early it's a Bow Street Runner!"

"Don't kick the blighter out until we're certain he's a dirty old man and not a very wealthy but slightly eccentric dealer."

China

Lovely stuff is china and very variable. It extends from solid lumps of Staffordshire pottery at the one end of the spectrum to the finest and most translucent Chinese porcelain at the other. You pays yer money and you takes yer choice. Prices often range from a few pounds to a few thousand pounds.

Chipped and damaged pieces have their attraction when you are learning to appreciate china but nothing can surpass the possession of an ornament, a cup or even a fairing that is perfect and undamaged. If you have damaged pieces in your collection you can always follow the example of my friend's elderly mother. To the casual eye she had an extraordinary collection of Meissen displayed in a large cabinet. Unfortunately each piece was damaged in one way or another and the old lady had turned each piece so its best side was on view.

This was a harmless subtefuge as she wasn't trying to sell the collection. The only person who was ever irked by this small deception was herself. She was waiting for a time when the family would become wealthy enough for each piece to be replaced. In the meantime she could at least appreciate her collection of porcelain until she came to dust it.

Hunting for a jewel of undamaged china whether it is at Boot Fairs or Antique Auctions is a pleasure in itself. You never know where you are likely to find such an objet d'art nor the lengths you would be prepared to go to possess it.

I was once with a good friend who discovered a large Worcestershire cheese dish at the Grass Market in Edinburgh. I still claim that I was the first to spot it hiding on a stall filled with cracked and chipped china. But once spied, she almost broke my wrist in getting to it first.

On a later occasion I found an inkstand on a stall in the Portabello Road which I cleaned up and gave away as a Christmas present. It transpired that it was a piece of Sevres. I now have the reputation, though accidentally earned, for being an exceptionally generous man. It is a nice reputation to have, but on reflection, I would rather have had the inkstand!

There are two lessons to be learned from these experiences. The first is to be sure you can recognise what you have in your hand and then hold on to it!

"The hallmark is almost certainly Jurassic."

"Are you looking for anything in particular, Ma'am, or do you merely wish to put sticky finger marks on the china I've spent all morning dusting?"

"He is an eccentric Californian gambler who owns a vast collection of crystal and fine china and chooses to live on the San Andreas Fault!"

"*What a wonderful record! In forty-three years the only things you've broken are the fingers of someone who handled your stock carelessly?*"

"Never refer to them as plates, my son. Call them tableware and they immediately become more collectable than functional."

"The only undamaged figurine I have is one of Nelson - and he's lacking an arm and an eye anyway!"

"It's a Meissen table centre. I bought it as a conversation piece but unfortunately it seems to cut off the flow of conversation altogether!"

*"This is either a fake or a priceless example of a piece far in advance of its time -
one sees very few Winston Churchill toby jugs dated 1850."*

"Eight hundred and sixty thousand - don't bother about the ninety-nine pence, your Highness."

"Would you like me to wrap that vase, sir, or will you be wearing it home?"

"I am arresting you for producing forged, free-range, Faberge eggs with intent to deceive."

"- a perfect example of a pre-war, nanny operated, Wedgewood potty."